September's Chronicle

AF624511

Charlotte Brown

BookLeaf Publishing

September's Chronicle © 2022 Charlotte Brown

All rights reserved.

No part of this publication may be reproduced, stored in a retrieval system, or transmitted, in any form or by any means, electronic, mechanical, photocopying, recording or otherwise, without the prior written permission of the presenters.

Charlotte Brown asserts the moral right to be identified as author of this work.

Presentation by *BookLeaf Publishing*

Web: www.bookleafpub.com

E-mail: info@bookleafpub.com

ISBN: 9789357445535

First edition 2022

DEDICATION

For my coven, who've read it all before and will hear it all again

PREFACE

As summer turns to autumn and the end of the year comes into sight, I find myself simultaneously in a period of reflection and looking forward. Bringing the events of the past year into order and already preparing for the one yet to come. It's also a time of harvest. When the abundance that was planted earlier comes to fruition and this is what we have here: an idea that has (finally) grown into a reality.

I

We say goodbye to Summer
Though its kiss was all too brief
We wrap ourselves for Winter
Ready to consolidate our grief
For now we live in Autumn
A mixture of joy and pain
And look towards the new year
When Spring will come again

II

As the summer leaves begin to turn
The earliest heralds of the autumnal winds
With covering clouds to match the mood
We sob goodbye to the precious flowers
The fresh and bright blooms have gone
Scared by the mere thought of cold
Now begins the harvest crop
With their glorious deep, rich colours
Winking from ground and gorse alike

III

What a feat of nature's engineering
That such sweet treasure
Might be secured behind as thin a fortress
The slightest pressure applied
And the juices leap forth
Hoping to stain a shirt, our hands or lips
This must be thought of in our collection
But looking across at you
I can see this will be no secret raid
All will know of our triumphant haul
The colour smeared from your mouth to mine
Your sticky fingers getting as caught in my hair
As the brambles clinging to your jumper
No matter
The hedgerows are a veritable trove today
And we are in no rush

IV

Yesterday the evening was longer
Tomorrow it will be shorter still
I haven't yet got my coats
Out of their summer storage
Maybe soon it will be time
How can the difference of a day
Make the seasons so keenly felt
The invisible threshold has been crossed
And we cannot go back

V

The slow transition from life
To the quiet deathly sleep
Of the bitter winter months
Is so incrementally small
That you might not see it at first
But the trees wave goodbye
To their leaves and to us
Their roots covered completely
By an autumnal blanket
They took all year to make
Given time it will disappear
Along with all the warm colours
Till the roots shiver for want of snow

VI

A brilliant day of sunshine
Warm enough to tease of summer
It's happened on a languid day
When we have little else to do
Save lying back and enjoying
Letting our bodies soak in the heat
Pretending that this surprise
Could possibly last for longer
All the while knowing
That this is a last hurrah

VII

I'm not sure what wakes me
But there is something different
The golden glow of sunrise
Creates a shining halo around the curtains
And holds a promise for the day to come
Despite the comfort of my downy cloud
There is no sluggishness to my movements
Or muffled moans for more sleep
This early dawn light is easier to greet
Than the full force of the noonday sun

VIII

If I were being honest
I don't mind the longer nights
The cold that requires fending off
With an army of blankets and cuddles
The food that warms the very soul
As it slips down your throat
Wind that bites at your face
Scarves pulled close to the skin
But with summer still clinging on
I should enjoy the heat
And simply dream of winter

IX

The sweltering heat of summer
Stifles the city once more
All the way to the crowded riverbanks
Everyone is searching for the smallest breath of air
Yet not a single one is to be found
Even with windows flung open wide
There are some brave few
Who roam the parks like children in search of a ball
With a dedication that soon fades away
Come evening the heavens finally sigh
The resulting downpour is the release we anticipated
But we bemoan it nonetheless

X

The rains of autumn
Are not like the ones that come in spring
Which promise growth and life
These rains instead bring the gloom of winter
Into every sodden step
This is the rain that could last forever
Till all the world is flooded
With only the tallest peaks and monumental relics
Able to be seen from our saviour arks

XI

The sky is sick of crying
The clouds have emptied their reserves
They relent some of their defences
Allowing the sunlight to trickle through
The weakly mirrored reflections
Shimmer on the pavement
Pools of water gather
Where both sets of feet meet
A glistening entrance to a world that's not our own

XII

Seasons in the countryside
Are different than in the city
Where the facades of artifice
Remain unaltered year round
With only the smallest hints of change
Desperately surviving in the the cracks
As we leave the choked streets behind
Nature expands to absorb us all
In her ever changing embrace
To show us how each day
Brings a different coloured leaf
A new blossom of fruit on the bramble
The skeletal trees that go easily unnoticed
In the skyscraper laden skies
Look barer on the hills out here
Where nothing else stands as tall

XIII

The coverings drop from the trees in the park
And fall into place around my neck
Weaving themselves into a scarf, a hat, and
gloves
I carry the warmth not found outside
And breathe it into my hands
The chill of the night taking longer to disperse
The dew still sits on the blades of grass
Who bow their heads with the weight
Waiting for the sun to eventually rise
And carry a warm wind through them
The peoples' heads are also lowered
Focussed on the now treacherous path
Steps must be placed securely
Else one might take a fall

XIV

The heather turns to gorse
And the grey rocks suddenly turn purple
Against the now brown heath covering them
The mountains grow imposing
Rows of teeth enclosing the calm loch
Where before they were protective
Winds whistle through the crags
And I remember the tales of wailing women
Who threw themselves upon these slopes
Maybe distant travellers only heard the wind
And there were never any broken girls
But stories told around a fire
Need a desperate end
To leave us clinging to our hearths
Or we'd all get lost out there

XV

The icy water sluices through my mental fog
No other thoughts can survive
Even my breath comes out ragged
But I feel more alive now than before
The physical urge to persist
Becomes a blaze within my soul
The dying trees on the banks look on
Jealous of my new lease of life
But their time will come
Winter is but a slow sleep
And spring a distant dream or memory
Until that first new gasp
Bursting through the seasons
Like the heart in my chest

XVI

The heat of summer is finally gone
The sun is now just a light
Hazy in the grey sky, no brilliance
There is scant warmth if you stand still
Even with the wind sitting low
Barely moving the few remaining leaves
That cling to their branches with a determination
Unrivalled in any human endeavour
And with the days getting shorter
We learn to greet the day with the moon
Still sitting above the horizon
Getting higher each day

XVII

I look into your eyes
Oases in this desert world
Teeming with as much life
As the hidden pools of the forest
Where no human hand has touched
But your step is of the fairies
Lighter than a brush of your lips
On the swirling rush of air
Carrying music from your throat
That calls back to the past
As if it could be changed
You look into my eyes
I wonder what you could see
If you are as enamoured
With a mortal such as me?

XVIII

Toss your ego out the window
It's as useful as a cloud
Only providing shade
When we are searching for the sun
Let it fall like autumn leaves
Discarded on the road
Don't think of what you can gain
But what others might share with you
There is something so much bigger
Than what our two eyes can see
So use both head and heart
Listen with every sense you possess
To the world as it continually spins
Maybe with the later snows
You'll forget that you were one
And think of all the good to be done
As part of a greater whole

XIX

I thought that I could change the world
The naïve belief of youth
That a single person would make a difference
Swept away by the cynicism of our elders
Who know so much more
So clearly know better
But now that I am older
And know more myself
I can see that a single rock
Over time can change the river's course
That one extra drop of snow
Will cause the avalanche to fall
And just one day sees the world
Turn from summer greens to rich browns
This causes me to think
About the dreams I used to have
And wonder if just maybe
I should start to dream again

XX

Here's the thing about cycles
They have a habit of ending
Of letting the close of play creep up
So slowly it happens all at once
We who are within
Don't see the changes start
And it's only when we step away
That the difference is startling on our return
Allow yourself a break
Let the seasons carry you along
Your evolution can be reflected
In the one the world goes through
Take a moment of evaluation
Tally up your scores
It matters not if it evens out
For you haven't finished yet
The other thing about cycles
Is that they start again
They have a chance to improve
The same is said for you

XXI

I see the path ahead of me
Get harder at every turn
Looking back at where I've walked
Nothing seemed this difficult
But I remember that I struggled
With certain steps along the way
So I know that I will survive
What the future has in store
Think of life as the seasons
Starting in the spring
When all the world seems hopeful
With limitless potential
And then we're into summer
With the gorgeous, carefree days
Not caring about what comes next
Or the troubles that may grow
Once we're in autumn
The fear becomes real
What once was only imagined
Jumps out in front of us
The falling leaves and swirling snows
Aim to block our progress
But the winter months can't last forever
That much we all know
So the steps that lie ahead

Might seem tougher now
But soon you'll be on smoother roads
When spring has come again

www.ingramcontent.com/pod-product-compliance
Lightning Source LLC
Chambersburg PA
CBHW051718130826
49812CB00034B/1244
9789357445535